The ABCs of Positive Parenting

The ABCs of Positive Parenting

A Creative Approach to Raising Children

written by
Julie D. Hunter

TATE PUBLISHING & Enterprises

Published by Tate Publishing & Enterprises, LLC
127 E. Trade Center Terrace | Mustang, Oklahoma 73064 USA
1.888.361.9473 | www.tatepublishing.com

Tate Publishing is committed to excellence in the publishing industry. The company reflects the philosophy established by the founders, based on Psalm 68:11,
"The Lord gave the word and great was the company of those who published it."

Published in the United States of America

ISBN: 978-1-61777-840-7
1. Family & Relationships / Parenting / Child Rearing
2. Family & Relationships / Parenting / General
11.06.06

Dedication

This book is dedicated to parents all over the world. I wish you smooth, positive parenting.

Foreword

"Stop crying."
"No hitting your sister."
"Stop talking back."
"Quit whining."
"Don't use that snotty tone with me."

I wrote this book to help remind myself and parents everywhere that if you take a more positive approach to discipline, your children will react in a more positive way. I myself, being a parent of two young children, found myself constantly spouting out these negative commands. From the time my daughter was born, I began to read several parenting books to help guide me though the tougher times (terrible twos or threes, incorporating another child into the family, or just coping with having kids in the house). From inspiring books such as *Happiest Toddler on the Block*, *Everyday Blessings*, *Time-out for Parents*, and many more, I gathered information to help me find different approaches to dealing with the several stages of my children's lives. I then read *The Secret* and *The Power*. Those two books completed the circle of information for me. It was there all along. I just realized if I changed the tone of my discipline from the "don't do that" tone to the "yes, do that" or "let's try it this way" tone, I could turn discipline into a more positive approach.

I would find myself struggling with my daughter, saying, "You're not listening to me," "Stop being snotty," or, "Stop talking back." And with my son, the typical commands would be, "Stop hitting your sister," "No sticking your tongue out," and, "No throwing." I now try a more positive approach and say instead, "Where are your listening ears?" "Where is your *nice* voice?" "Show me your nice hands." I realized that if I focus on the negative aspects of my children, I will receive more of it. However, if I focus on a more positive approach, I will receive more positive actions from my children. We have our days, but if I try to remember to focus on love and take a calmer, positive approach, the days always seem more pleasant and the memories last a lifetime.

Awareness:

Awareness is the key. It is the beginning and end. Once you are aware, everything will fall into place.

I do my best to start the day with an awareness of my mood and my children's moods. If I can start out aware at the beginning of a situation, I can usually come up with a creative idea to keep it from becoming a disaster.

Behavior:

Behave how you want your child to behave. You are their primary teacher.

Children will learn from every move you make. They will copy your words, actions, and tone. The best way to teach them love and patience is to be loving and patient.

Consistency:

Children need to know what to expect from their parents. Then they are aware of their boundaries.

Children love a routine. When they know what is coming next, they deal with the situation better and feel more in control because they know the next step. My family has a morning routine and a nighttime routine. That way, when I give my five-minute warnings for things like dinnertime, teeth time, or bedtime, they are less likely to become irritated.

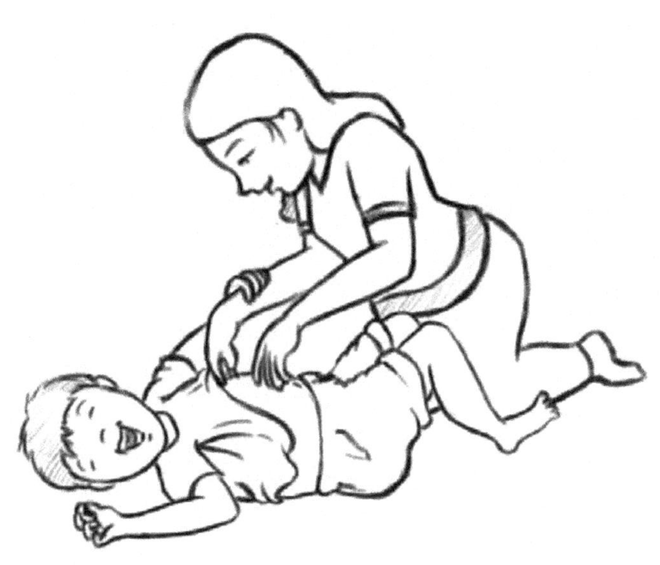

Diversions:

Change the subject or activity when tempers flare.

My favorite diversions work with younger children. It is easy to divert an upset child with a different toy, a funny game like the tickle monster, or just by being silly. Older children might need to be directed to a different room for some special time with or without you.

Energy:

When your energy is good, your child's will be too. The calmer you are, the calmer they are.

On days when I feel frazzled, in a rush, or have an agenda of my own (usually simply trying to vacuum or mop), my children feel that energy and are wound up tight or just seem cranky. If I focus my energy completely on them and do so calmly, they usually end up very involved with an activity and I can accomplish my mission.

Flexible:

Let your child win some battles. This increases confidence and gives you the energy to focus on winning the more important battles.

When I find myself in a situation, struggling to gain control, and realize the battle is a pretty small one, I will quietly back off and say, "Okay. You can stay up for five more minutes." The glowing smile on my daughter's face makes up for the loss of this small battle.

OOKIES

Guidance:

Provide the foundation for making good decisions or dealing with the consequences of making bad decisions.

I believe it is important to teach my children to always tell the truth, even if they made a bad decision. I also have them apologize if they make a bad decision. I myself make bad decisions and *always* apologize to my children when I am in the wrong or have overreacted.

Humor:

Make up a goofy story, act silly, or pretend to be your child's favorite superhero or princess when you're dealing with a battle. This can sometimes dissolve the entire issue.

When my two-year-old is throwing a temper tantrum about something (usually everything), I sometimes copy his noises, which sound very silly coming from an adult. This stops him in his tracks and makes him giggle. I then repeat a silly noise, and before you know it, we are both giggling *and* the situation is diffused by me already dealing with the problem, such as switching toys, washing hands, or leaving the park.

Interact:

Be a part of your child's everyday life. Talk, sing, read. They learn from you.

It's sometimes hard to set aside a large amount of time to spend with your children when you work, parent, and keep up the house. But it is easy to incorporate time into the day by singing songs during cleanup, going over the day during dinner, and learning letters and numbers in the car or body parts while changing diapers.

Joy:

Happiness leads to laughter. Laughter is life's remedy to all ailments.

Kindness:

Be kind to your child, and your child will learn to be kind to you.

We have all been caught off guard by our little ones repeating something we said. They are like little sponges, and we are their water.

Love:

Just love.

"All you need is love" (The Beatles).

"That's the power of love" (Huey Lewis and the News).

Motivate:

Teach your child about taking care of chores, the house, and pets. They will better understand and appreciate what it takes to run a household.

My children love to help out as long as it's fun. So we will all pitch in together to help clean while we sing "clean up as we go." The whole family is singing and cleaning together. I also insist that we "clean up as we go" before starting a new game, project, or play center. That way they are motivated to clean before they can start something new. (This helps keep the house a bit tidier too.)

Nurture:

Provide the support and encouragement your children need in every situation as they grow and learn.

I make it a point to praise the positive every time, *especially* if I only had to ask once or the task was completed without my even asking. I make a *huge* deal out of a task completed without a hassle.

Options:

Let your child make some of their own decisions. This builds confidence.

I will allow my children to make their own choices. There are several choices children can make that make them feel in control. I always limit choices to two or three. Simple choices such as milk or juice, this dress or that one, strawberries or bananas, make children feel more in control of their environment.

Patience:

I am constantly practicing patience.

I find that the easiest way to be patient is to first be aware.

Quality:

Set specific time aside to spend quality time with your children.

We call the weekend "family days." We talk about how long until our "family days" all week. Before I set out to catch up on all the housework, we set aside family time in the morning. During the week, we have "movie kick-it time." It is loudly announced through the house after bath. This is our time as a family to sit together. It's our quiet-down time. After brushing teeth we have "happy thoughts," where we spend ten minutes listing all the things that make us happy. These set quality times are very well known with the children, and they look forward to the quality time we all spend together.

GREAT
JOB

Rewards:

Offer rewards for good behavior and being a good helper.

Star charts, hand stamps, and stickers are like magic signs that encourage good behavior. If your child can visibly see that they are doing a good job, they will want to continue their good behavior. Rewards can be used for potty training, good listening, good behavior all day—just about anything you are trying to encourage (or discourage by using the positive side of the behavior).

Stories:

Make-believe stories are a fun way to encourage your child to do something he or she doesn't want to do.

You can make up a story for just about any struggle you are having with your child. Brushing teeth is a common struggle in our house. I will say, "Eww. I have to get those sugar bugs. There is an entire family living in there," or, "Oh wow. Today I see food goobers. Hurry. I have to get them before they go to sleep." I will change the story weekly to keep it interesting. For my older child, fairy and princess stories work great for sleeping problems. I will often sprinkle happy sleepy fairy dust all over her bed to ensure happy dreams.

Tactful:

Be tactful about your approach to different children. Different personalities require different approaches to a situation.

My daughter is very sensitive, while my son can be easily diverted with humor. I usually have to use two different approaches to resolve a situation. Part is age, but most is personality. With my daughter, I find a lot more explanation and guidance is needed. However, my son only needs a quick tickle and a hug, and he is off playing.

Understand:

Understand and hear where your child is coming from. They might have a different point of view worth talking about.

During the heat of the moment, it is easy to be distracted with whining, tears, or temper tantrums, especially after a long day at work. I sometimes find myself getting upset at whining before really hearing the problem. If I take the time out to carefully listen and understand the problem before reacting to it, there is usually a very easy solution (such as my daughter just wanted her hair out of her face instead of the perfect ponytail).

Validate:

If your child is upset, validate their feelings. Let them know that you understand what they are saying or why they are upset.

When I say to my children, "I know you don't want to get out of bed," "I know you don't want to wash your hands for dinner," or, "I know you don't want to clean up your toys," this lets them know that I *hear* what they are saying. This tends to change their mood enough so I can use another creative tactic, such as a silly story about the germs on their hands.

Warnings:

Give your child advance time warnings as often as possible.

I do my best to give time warnings before dinner, bed, naptime, or any other activity I know might prompt a battle. A five-minute warning before such activities gives your child warnings so you don't catch them off guard. This will help them better accept the activity when it arrives.

XOXOX:

Lots of hugs and kisses. We all need them.

You:

Love and take care of yourself. The more you do that, the easier it is to love and take care of someone else.

When I take time out for myself, I am more aware, more positive, and have more patience for my children.

Zen:

Be enlightened by everything your child does. They can be your very best teachers.

There is no better way to learn than to be put in the situation and deal with it in a more positive way. Once I realized this positive approach produced results, I was determined to try it over and over again. My children have been my best teachers.

Ingram Content Group UK Ltd.
Milton Keynes UK
UKHW051004140723
425124UK00008B/52